PARABLES

PORTRAITS OF GOD'S KINGDOM IN MATTHEW, MARK, AND LUKE

Other studies in the Not Your Average Bible Study series

Ruth

Psalms

Jonah

Malachi

Sermon on the Mount

Romans

Ephesians

Philippians

Colossians

Hebrews

James

1 Peter

2 Peter and Jude

1–3 John

PARABLES

PORTRAITS OF GOD'S KINGDOM IN MATTHEW, MARK, AND LUKE

NOT YOUR AVERAGE BIBLE STUDY

JOHN D. BARRY

LEXHAM PRESS

Parables: Portraits of God's Kingdom in Matthew, Mark, and Luke
Not Your Average Bible Study

Adapted with permission from content published in *Bible Study Magazine* (Volume 10, Issues 5–6, and Volume 11, Issues 1–2).

Lexham Press, 1313 Commercial St., Bellingham, WA 98225
LexhamPress.com

Scripture quotations are the author's own translation.

Print ISBN 9781683592570
Digital ISBN 9781683592587

Lexham Editorial Team: David Bomar, Danielle Thevenaz
Cover Design: Brittany Schrock
Typesetting: Abigail Stocker

CONTENTS

HOW TO USE
THIS RESOURCE

Not Your Average Bible Study is a series of in-depth Bible studies that can be used for individual or group study. The content and format are flexible. You can work through the study guide daily or weekly, according to your individual needs or your group pace.

Each lesson prompts you to dig deep into God's word. We recommend you use your preferred translation with this study (which was written based on the author's own translation). Whatever Bible version you use, please be sure you leave ample time to get into the Bible itself.

To assist you, we recommend using the Faithlife Study Bible. You can download this digital resource for your tablet, phone, personal computer, or use it online. Go to FaithlifeBible.com to learn more.

May God bless you in the study of his word.

INTRODUCTION

What is the kingdom of heaven?

Jesus says the kingdom of heaven is *like* a mustard seed. The smallest of seeds becomes a great plant that birds can use for nests. Jesus says the kingdom of heaven is *like* a man who found a treasure in a field and in joy sold everything he had to buy that field. The kingdom of heaven is *like* leaven to flour—it raises the entire loaf of bread (all these examples are from Matthew 13).

But Jesus never says the kingdom of heaven *is* any of these things. That's because the kingdom of heaven is a great mystery.

The mystery of the kingdom is reflected in the mystery of Jesus' parables. In this Bible study, we will survey parables from across Jesus' three years in ministry.

These parables are found in Matthew, Mark, and Luke, which are called the Synoptic Gospels because they follow similar outlines and can be read alongside each other (Greek: *syn*=together; *optic*=seeing). Each week's reading focuses on one of the Synoptic Gospels, but we'll also look at parallel passages.

Let's journey together into Jesus' stories as he reveals to us what the kingdom of heaven is like.

PART 1

THE KINGDOM TAKES ROOT

How do we recognize the kingdom of heaven? What does it look and feel like? Can we see glimpses of it here on earth?

When Jesus teaches about the kingdom of heaven, he often speaks in parables, which can be short metaphors, extended metaphors, or similes. A simile is when we compare one thing to another or say something is *like* another thing:

> The kingdom of heaven is like a merchant searching for precious pearls; and finding a very valuable pearl, he sold everything he owned and bought it. (Matt 13:45–46)

Jesus also tells stories that compare and contrast the common values of society to how the kingdom of heaven works; these are another type of parable.

In the New Testament, the phrase "kingdom of heaven" is synonymous with "kingdom of God." So the parables reveal what the kingdom of heaven is all about: God's reign (his perfect will) coming to earth as it is in heaven (Matt 6:10).

NEW CLOTH +
NEW WINESKINS

Pray that Jesus would reveal a portion of the mystery of the kingdom of heaven to you.

Read Matthew 9:14–17 and Mark 2:18–22. Then read and reflect on Luke 5:33–39.

These passages are set during Jesus' ministry in Galilee, the region where he grew up. The Pharisees—who ask Jesus the question that leads to him telling these parables—were big on procedure, particularly when it came to the laws in Exodus to Deuteronomy. What does this context indicate about their inquiry?

_____

_____

_____

What does the parallel passage of Revelation 19:6–9 indicate about the meaning of Luke 5:33–34?

_____

_____

_____

What two words do the two parables in Luke 5:36–39 share in common?

_____

_____

_____

Think for a moment about why you would *never* tear a new piece of cloth and place it on an old one, aside from the obvious result of ruining the new fabric (5:36). What is the difference between a new pair of jeans and an old pair in terms of flexibility? What would likely happen if a new piece of denim were used to sow up a tear at the knee of an old pair of jeans?

_____

_____

_____

_____

In Jesus' day, containers made from animal skins were used to store wine. As new wine fermented, the wineskins would expand and flex. Since old wineskins had already been used during the fermentation process, the gases of new wine could cause them to explode. Keep in mind that Jesus is responding to a question about long periods of fasting and prayer—and why his disciples don't regularly observe this practice like the Pharisees. What does Jesus' Parable of Wineskins have to do with fasting (5:37-38)? Note that Jesus is not opposing fasting and prayer, but speaking to a specific context when he is present with his disciples.

_____

_____

_____

_____

THE BUILDER +
THE LAMP UNDER A BASKET

Pray that Jesus would help you show other people the kingdom of God.

Read Matthew 5:14-16; 7:24-27; Mark 4:21-25. Then read and reflect on Luke 6:46-49; 8:16-18; 11:33-36.

The Parable of the Builder is part of Jesus' most pivotal sermon, known as the Sermon on the Mount (Matt 5-7) or the Sermon on the Plain (Luke 6:17-49). This sermon represents the core of Jesus' teachings on what it means to be part of the kingdom of God (or kingdom of heaven). The Parable of the Builder is the conclusion of the sermon.

Jesus compares our lives to the building of a house (Luke 6:46-49). If your life were a home, what would be the foundation? Or, what *should* be the foundation? (6:46).

_____

_____

_____

What is a person *like* who doesn't listen to Jesus' teachings (6:49)? What is a person's spiritual life like when it is built on the wrong principles? How does a person's spiritual life affect their mental health and response to crisis (the rising water)?

_____

_____

_____

Examine Luke 8:16–18 in light of 6:46–49. If you observe Jesus' teachings, what will other people witness (8:16)? A lamp in Jesus' time referred to a flame powered by oil.

_____

_____

_____

How is the kingdom of heaven revealed to people for the first time (Luke 8:16–17)? Jesus' message may also have another meaning: Ultimately, sin is always revealed or addressed (Matt 10:26).

_____

_____

_____

If we observe Jesus' principles, what are the results (Luke 8:18)? If we ignore them—if we're "the one who has not"—what will be the result?

_____

_____

_____

THE TWO DEBTORS

Pray that God would reveal to you the weight of sin and what it means to be free.

Read Luke 7:36-50. Then reflect slowly on 7:41-48; doing so will help you internalize Jesus' message.

What does the context of this parable say about its meaning? What prompts Jesus to offer this parable (Luke 7:36-40)? Consider that the Pharisees greatly valued purity and generally viewed touching a "sinner" as having a defiling effect. Also keep this in mind: Even though Jesus was viewed as a prophetic rabbi, this episode takes place in his home region of Galilee, where people were skeptical of him as the hometown kid (Luke 4:24; John 6:42; Matt 13:53-58).

In Jesus' parable, what is sin *like?* (What's it analogous to?) Who is the woman in the parable? Who is Simon? See Luke 7:44-46.

_____

_____

_____

_____

_____

How does a person's perception of their own sinfulness affect their ability to love others (7:47)?

_____

_____

_____

Is Simon's perception of himself (and his sin) accurate or misguided? Simon was likely a valuable member of the Jewish community whose life was marked by the public perception that he was a pure and righteous Pharisee who kept the Jewish law.

_____

_____

_____

What does the woman *do* that makes her different from Simon? What do her actions show (especially see Jesus' statement in 7:50)?

_____

_____

_____

How should we each view our own sinfulness (debt), and how should we act as members of the kingdom (who are forgiven)?

_____

_____

_____

THE SOWER

Pray that the seed of God's kingdom would grow in your heart.

Read Mark 4:1–20; compare Matthew 13:1–23; Luke 8:4–15. Then reflect slowly on Mark 4:1–9.

Why does Jesus speak in parables to the crowd, but not to his disciples (Mark 4:10–11)? In Mark 4:12, Jesus paraphrases Isaiah 6:9–10, in which God tells Isaiah that those who have already rejected God should be allowed to continue on their path. Jesus is essentially telling his disciples that those who refuse to hear God's message of repentance—and who reject salvation through the Messiah, Jesus—will experience the path of judgment they have chosen (compare John 3:17). But to those who receive Jesus (his disciples), the mystery of God's kingdom is revealed. They *understand* the parables. They move beyond *hearing* them to *observing* Jesus' teachings and *experiencing* what the kingdom of heaven means.

The Parable of the Sower—which Jesus delivered in Galilee (his home region)—is one of the few parables he explains in detail (Mark 4:13–20). What does Jesus' explanation teach us about how to interpret his other parables?

_____

_____

_____

_____

Who is the sower (4:13–14)? What are the various ways the sower could sow seed?

_____

_____

_____

In the parable, which of the four types of people truly experience the mystery of God's kingdom (4:15-20)? What stands in the way of the other people? What can each of them do to ensure they become active members of the kingdom of God? (Did some of them even contemplate the ramifications of their decision to accept or reject Jesus?)

_____

_____

_____

_____

_____

For those who experience the kingdom of God, what is the expectation? (See 4:21-25 and reflect on your insights from Lesson 2.)

_____

_____

_____

_____

THE SEED THAT GROWS

Pray that the seeds of God's kingdom would grow like weeds—everywhere.

Read and reflect on Mark 4:26-29.

Jesus offered the Parable of the Seed that grows while in his home region of Galilee. His appeal to how God's kingdom grows mysteriously—like a man who simply scatters seed on the ground and watches it grow—is a subtle rebuke to those in Galilee who rejected his message. This parable could be read as Jesus saying, "This will happen no matter how you respond."

The Parable of the Sower (Mark 4:1-20) suggests that the *seed* in verses 26-29 represents God's word—the saving message of Jesus (4:14). But note that the perspective has changed in the Parable of the Seed That Grows. Jesus is now speaking about his disciples' mission to spread his teachings.

In light of the mysterious nature of the kingdom of God, should we worry if our ministries don't seem to be working? Does the sower worry (4:27)?

_____

_____

_____

_____

Think about how the seed sprouts (4:28-29). What does this symbolize in terms of a person's life? Especially consider this question in light of the Parable of the Sower. (See Mark 4:1-20 and reflect on your insights from Lesson 4.)

_____

_____

_____

Consider the Parable of the Seed That Grows from the perspective of your neighborhood or city. What would a harvest look like in this broader context? How should we go about our ministry efforts?

_____

_____

_____

_____

THE BARREN FIG TREE

Pray that God would help your life be a blessing to others.

Read and reflect on Luke 13:6–9.

Consider the context of this parable in Luke: Jesus has just been told of Pontius Pilate (Roman governor of Judea) killing two Galileans while they were offering sacrifices in Jerusalem (Luke 13:1). To explain this event, Jesus mentions another recent tragedy (13:4). Jesus uses both events to make the point that everyone will experience God's judgment. These tragedies emphasize the need to repent, for we never know what day is our last (13:5). In light of this context, what is the point of the Parable of the Barren Fig Tree?

_____

_____

_____

_____

Consider Jesus' final remark in Luke 13:8–9, then read 2 Peter 3:8–10. Taken together, what do these passages indicate about God's timing, grace, and judgment?

_____

_____

_____

_____

Read Mark 11:12–25. What does the fig tree illustrate in this instance?

_____

_____

_____

What is God's expectation for his people—for our lives? How should members of the kingdom of heaven live?

_____

_____

_____

_____

THE GOOD FIG TREE

Pray that God would give you courage to do his will, no matter how hard things get.

Read Matthew 24:32–36; Luke 21:29–33. Then read and reflect on Mark 13:28–32.

Just before Jesus tells the Parable of the Good Fig Tree (Mark 13:28–32), he has been discussing issues concerning his return to earth—when the final judgment of all of humanity will take place and all things will be restored and renewed (13:1–31). He discusses these things during his last days in Jerusalem, a time leading up to his death on the cross.

Jesus particularly emphasizes the difficulties of the last times—which began when he ascended to heaven (after his resurrection) and continue today. Jesus also stresses that no one will be able to predict the day of his return. In light of all this, what's the purpose of the Parable of the Good Fig Tree (13:28–32)?

_____

_____

_____

What do the branches extending out signify about the season we're living in? What is God doing in this period? (Consider Luke 13:6–9 and your insights from Lesson 6.)

_____

_____

_____

When Jesus refers to the generation not passing away until these things have taken place, he is referring to the era before God's kingdom is fully established—that is, he is talking about the generation we're currently living in (Mark 13:30). In light of this, what is the significance of Jesus' parables in general (13:31)? What do they teach us about how to live between now and when he returns?

_____

_____

_____

COUNTING THE COST

Pray that Jesus would give you the courage to make sacrifices for the sake of the kingdom of heaven.

Read Luke 14:25–35; compare Matthew 10:37–38. Then reflect slowly on Luke 14:26–33.

What is the cost of being a member of the kingdom of heaven? How does it cost us in terms of our resources and our relationships? What is the value of the kingdom of heaven in comparison to everything else (see Matthew 13)?

_____

_____

_____

Read 1 Corinthians 1:20–25. What cost has Jesus paid for us to be members of the kingdom of God? (Compare Luke 23:26–24:12.)

_____

_____

_____

Read Luke 9:57–62. What does this reveal about the commitment Jesus expects his followers to have toward him and the kingdom of heaven?

_____

_____

_____

Read Luke 14:34-35 (compare Matt 5:13 and Mark 9:49-50). What happens if a person does not count the cost and take action for Jesus? What are they *like*?

_____

_____

_____

In contrast, will more of the mystery of the kingdom be revealed to those who sacrifice more for Jesus—those who count the cost and deem it worthwhile?

_____

_____

_____

CONCLUSION

The parables we've examined are organic and practical, with imagery from agriculture and finance. But they signify the great mystery of the kingdom of heaven. They reveal to us what it's like for God's presence to reclaim the brokenness of our world. For these reasons, Jesus ultimately asks us to *count the cost* and observe God's word. Our sins have been forgiven and we can celebrate with Jesus the bridegroom. And why wouldn't we? Let's live like we're part of God's kingdom.

PART 2

THE KINGDOM IS PRESENT WITH US

What is God like? Can we predict him? Jesus describes God's Spirit as something that comes and goes like the wind (John 3:8). Like the wind, we don't know where the Spirit is coming from or where it's going. But like the wind, we can feel God's presence. And it changes absolutely everything.

To come to an authentic understanding of God and his ways, we must be ready to experience his presence. Jesus says he spoke in parables for this very reason. Parables are extended metaphors or similes. When a person is ready to receive Jesus' message, the parables move from being riddles to being life lessons (Matt 13:10-17, 34-35). The stories or similes suddenly make sense of the kingdom of heaven—God's reign—and what it's all about.

What this all means is that to *understand* Jesus' parables, we have to *live* them. Or as Jesus puts it, we will truly *see* and *hear* his words about the kingdom of heaven *as* we learn to observe and live them (Mark 4:10-12, 33-34; Luke 8:9-10).

In these eight lessons, we will examine a series of parables Jesus delivered in Galilee, the region where he grew up; we will then look at four parables he delivered during his last journey to Jerusalem and the cross.

THE WEEDS AND THE WHEAT

Pray that Jesus would reveal to you how to follow him in a world that opposes him.

Read Matthew 13:24–43. Reflect on Matthew 13:24–30, 36–43. Taking time to reexamine what you've already read will help you internalize the message.

Jesus delivered this parable in Galilee, his home region, just after he told the Parable of the Sower (Matt 13:3–23). What does the Parable of the Weeds and the Wheat (13:24–30) have to do with the Parable of the Sower?

_____

_____

_____

How would Jesus being the hometown kid influence the perception of the original audience? Who would they have thought he was talking about? Keep in mind that Jesus was mostly rejected in his home region (Luke 4:24; John 6:42; Matt 13:53–58).

_____

_____

_____

This is one of the few parables Jesus explains in detail. In Matthew 13:36–43, he explains its meaning. Who are the characters and what do their various actions tell us about how God operates in the world today?

_____

_____

_____

What does it tell us about how evil operates in the world today?

_____

_____

_____

When Jesus speaks of the "close (or end) of the age," he is referring to when he will return to earth (13:39). What does Jesus say will happen in this time to those who know him (the righteous) and to those who have refused his offer of a relationship with God (13:39–43)?

_____

_____

_____

Note that Jesus directly connects the removal of those who embrace lawless deeds with the removal of the causes of sin (Matt 13:41). In light of this, what is God accomplishing in final judgment of the world?

_____

_____

_____

Read 2 Peter 2:9–13. What does God ultimately desire? Why has Jesus not yet returned to judge the world (2 Pet 2:9)?

_____

_____

_____

THE MUSTARD SEED +
THE YEAST

Pray that Jesus would reveal to you what the kingdom of heaven is like.

Read Matthew 13:31–33; Mark 4:30–32; Luke 13:18–21. Now slowly reflect on Mark 4:30–32 and Luke 13:20–21.

In Matthew's Gospel, the Parables of the Mustard Seed and the Yeast come just after Jesus tells the Parable of the Weeds and Wheat but before he explains it (Matt 13:24–30, 36–43). What is the relationship between these parables? What themes do they share? How are they different? Also compare Lesson 1, where we examined how the Parable of the Weeds and Wheat relates to the Parable of the Sower (13:3–23). In Matthew, these four parables are in the same sermon, along with four others (13:44–52; see Lessons 3 and 4).

_____

_____

_____

Based on Mark 4:30, 33–34, why did Jesus speak in parables?

_____

_____

_____

Like the kingdom of heaven (or kingdom of God), what does the mustard seed do? How is it a benefit and what is its behavior like (Mark 4:31–32)?

_____

_____

_____

Read Luke 13:10-17. When Jesus tells the Parables of the Mustard Seed and the Yeast in Luke's Gospel, what is the context (Luke 13:18-21)? What is the relationship between these parables and the events that occur right before and after?

_____

_____

_____

What is relationship between the Parable of the Mustard Seed and the Parable of the Yeast (Luke 13:18-21)? What is similar about a mustard seed and yeast? (Think specifically of the difference they make.) What does this suggest about how the kingdom of heaven works in our world and lives?

_____

_____

_____

THE HIDDEN TREASURE + THE VALUABLE PEARL

Pray that the Holy Spirit would help you be more self-sacrificial in your relationships and interactions.

Read Matthew 13:44–52. Contemplate the meaning of Matthew 13:44–46. Rereading a passage can help you identify things you didn't see before.

How does the man react to what he finds in the field (Matt 13:44)? What does this indicate about how we should react to Jesus' teachings—and to whatever God asks us to do?

_____

_____

_____

Read Matthew 19:16–30 (commonly called the story of the Rich Young Man). What does this indicate about the meaning of the Parable of the Hidden Treasure (13:44)? What does Jesus ultimately ask of us?

_____

_____

_____

What are some signs that we're members of the kingdom of heaven?

_____

_____

_____

According to the Parable of the Valuable Pearl, what is the value of the kingdom of heaven (13:45-46)? What does this indicate about the difference between someone who has truly experienced the kingdom of heaven and the person who has not?

_____

_____

_____

What are some key indicators of truly being members of the kingdom (Christians)?

_____

_____

_____

THE FISHING NET + NEW AND OLD TREASURES

Pray that Jesus would inspire you to live as one who fully embraces the kingdom of heaven.

Read Matthew 13:44–52. Reflect on Matthew 13:47–52. The more you read Jesus' words, the more his message will take root in your heart.

Consider the Parables of the Hidden Treasure and the Valuable Pearl (Matt 13:44–46). What is the relationship between these parables and the Parable of the Fishing Net (13:47–50)? Reflect on your insights from Lesson 3.

_____

_____

_____

Reread Matthew 13:24–30, 36–43 (the Parable of the Weeds and Wheat) and reflect on Lesson 1. What parallels do you see between this parable and the Parable of the Fishing Net (13:47–50)?

_____

_____

_____

Read Matthew 25:31–46. What is the visible sign of someone who knows Jesus? What is the difference between them and someone who does not know Jesus?

_____

_____

_____

What is the practical application of this teaching in our lives? How should we live in light of this truth? (Compare Luke 14:26-33.)

_____

_____

_____

In the Parable of New and Old Treasures (Matt 13:51-52), the "new" refers to Jesus' teachings; the "old" refers to the Old Testament Scriptures. Jesus is reinterpreting the Old Testament through the lens of his teachings on the kingdom of heaven. In light of this, what is the meaning of the Parable of New and Old Treasures? How should we explain the message of Jesus to other people?

_____

_____

_____

THE LOST SHEEP

Pray that God would reveal his overwhelming love to you—and show you how he loves everyone.

Read Matthew 18:10–14. Read and reflect on Luke 15:1–7.

In Matthew's Gospel, Jesus offers the Parable of the Lost Sheep during the time just prior to his crucifixion, often called the *Journey to the Cross*. In light of this context, read Matthew 18:1–9. What does this discussion indicate about the meaning of the parable in Matthew's context? (Keep in mind that children were often marginalized in the ancient Near East and seen as having little social value, outside of work.) What is Jesus teaching us about what it means to follow him? Where should our focus be?

_____

_____

_____

In Luke's Gospel, what is the complaint of the religious establishment that leads to Jesus telling the Parable of the Lost Sheep (Luke 15:1–2)?

_____

_____

_____

How does Jesus answer their objection (15:3–6)? What's the difference between his perspective and theirs?

_____

_____

_____

Read Luke 15:8–32 (the Parables of the Lost Coin and Lost Son). What is the relationship between these two parables and the Parable of the Lost Sheep?

_____

_____

_____

What is God's perspective on the sinner (the lost)—the person who is far from God (Luke 15:7)?

_____

_____

_____

Read John 3:16–17 and Romans 6:22–23. How is the sinner, who has yet to accept Jesus, lost in this life?

_____

_____

_____

Who is the shepherd, and what answers does he offer?

_____

_____

_____

THE UNFORGIVING SERVANT

Pray that God would teach the full meaning of forgiveness.

Read and reflect on Matthew 18:23–35.

In Matthew's Gospel, Jesus tells the Parable of the Unforgiving Servant shortly after the Parable of the Lost Sheep (Matt 18:10–14). (Compare Lesson 5, where it was noted that Jesus gave this parable during his *Journey to the Cross*.) What is the relationship between these two parables? (Note that the lost sheep never seems to resist the shepherd or his ways.)

_____

_____

_____

Read Matthew 18:15–22, where Jesus offers teaching between the two parables. What does this passage indicate about the meaning of the Parable of the Unforgiving Servant (18:23–35)? What issue is Jesus addressing (18:35)?

_____

_____

_____

What does the master do for the servant and why (Matt 18:27)? Does the servant (or "slave," in some translations) earn this? (The only action the servant takes is to show remorse—and only when he realizes the suffering he will face.)

_____

_____

_____

How are you like the servant?

_____

_____

_____

Read Romans 2. What is God's view of judging others and believing they owe us something? What is God's view of our own debt against him and others? Why are we indebted to God and others?

_____

_____

_____

Jesus offers free forgiveness from sin (our wrongdoings)—a concept known as *grace* (Rom 1:16–17). What does Matthew 18:23–35 indicate about how we should respond to this forgiveness? What should characterize our relationships with other people?

_____

_____

_____

THE GOOD SAMARITAN

Pray that Jesus would show you what it means to love your neighbor.

Read Luke 10:25–37. Reflect on Luke 10:30–37.

When the events of Luke 10:25–37 took place, Jesus was on his last journey to Jerusalem (where he would be crucified). This means he is reaching the close of his teachings; it is in this context that he tells the Parable of the Good Samaritan. What question is Jesus asked that ultimately leads to him telling this parable (10:25)?

_____

_____

_____

What does the parable indicate about how Jesus defines what it means to love God and other people (10:26–28)?

_____

_____

_____

What is Jesus' answer to the question of "who is my neighbor" (10:29)?

_____

_____

_____

What do we learn in verse 29 about the emotional state of the lawyer (or expert in the law)? How is this juxtaposed against the response of the Samaritan (10:33)?

_____

_____

_____

The man Jesus is speaking with is an expert in the Jewish Law (the first five books of the Bible). Jewish people in Jesus' time generally hated Samaritans with intense racism and viewed them as religiously incorrect. But in Jesus' parable, a Samaritan is a compassionate hero. In contrast, the priest and the Levite—two Jewish religious leaders—are depicted as ignoring the suffering man (10:31-32). In light of this, what is Jesus trying to accomplish with this parable?

_____

_____

_____

What action does the Samaritan take at the end of the story that we can emulate (10:35-37)? What does this action, and the Samaritan's other actions, show about how Jesus wants us to treat other people?

_____

_____

_____

What is the kingdom of heaven _like_ in light of this parable?

_____

_____

_____

THE FRIEND WHO ASKS

Pray that the Holy Spirit would reveal the mystery of God's kingdom.

Read Luke 11:1-13. Reflect on Luke 11:5-13.

During Jesus' last journey to Jerusalem (prior to his crucifixion), he offers the Parable of the Friend Who Asks (Luke 11:5-13). What does Jesus' teaching on prayer in Luke 11:1-4 have to do with the Parable of the Friend Who Asks?

_____

_____

_____

How does God respond to our prayers? What should characterize our prayers and determine how often we ask God for help (11:8)?

_____

_____

_____

What does the parable teach us about how should we respond to other people's needs (11:5-8)?

_____

_____

_____

Luke 11:9–10 is not meant to imply that God will always give us what we ask. Instead, God will always answer according to what is best for us (11:11–13). In light of this, how should we pray? What should we expect from God?

_____

_____

_____

What does Jesus say God the Father will ultimately give us (Luke 11:13)? Read John 14:15–21, which is about this same topic. What should be our expectations about this gift?

_____

_____

_____

If we want to experience the kingdom of heaven (God's reign), how should we respond to God? What should characterize our lives? What should be our focus and hope?

_____

_____

_____

CONCLUSION

The more you *experience* the kingdom of heaven—the more you accept all it entails—the more you *understand* it. You move from head knowledge to experiential knowledge. You begin going out of your way to be there for people—even those who can give nothing back. You begin living self-sacrificially, for the sake of our world. You pray for our world to become a better place and to *know* the God you pray to. You understand the kingdom of God by *living it*. Go *do* something that brings a little of heaven to earth.

PART 3

THE KINGDOM COMES ALIVE IN US

You can read Jesus' parables hundreds of times and mystery will still remain. That's part of what makes these teachings so beautiful—and powerful.

Jesus uses parables—metaphors and similes—to help us understand who God is and how he works among us. Through these parables, we understand God as Father, God as Son (Jesus), and God as Spirit. These parables teach us how to live for Jesus each day—how to be members of the kingdom of God.

Jesus' parables can be truly understood only when we *experience* their value in our lives. To understand God and his kingdom, we have to commit our lives to Jesus as his disciples and accept him as savior (John 3:16–17). From there, God as Holy Spirit will work in us. God may be ultimately unknowable, but he certainly can work in us. And we can see the wonder of his work reflected in other people.

In the first seven lessons of this section, we will examine ten parables Jesus delivered during his last journey to Jerusalem and just before his crucifixion. In the eighth lesson, we will look at one more parable he delivered in Judea a little earlier in his ministry.

These parables teach us about the mystery of living as people who, through our actions, bring heaven to earth. They teach us what it means to live as people who truly follow Jesus.

THE RICH FOOL

Pray that God would show you the true value of wealth.

Read Luke 12:13–21. Then reflect slowly on Luke 12:16–21.

What does the dialogue leading up to the Parable of the Rich Fool tell us about its meaning and purpose (Luke 12:13–15)? What is its core lesson?

_____

_____

_____

_____

Where does the rich man in Jesus' parable go wrong (12:16–21)?

_____

_____

_____

What can wealth do for you, and what can it *not* do (12:20–21)?

_____

_____

_____

Read Luke 12:22–34. How does Jesus expect people to respond to the kingdom of God?

_____

_____

_____

What is Jesus' view of wealth and how we should respond to wealth (Luke 12:15)? How can we be "rich toward God" (or "rich with God," which is another way to translate the original Greek)? What is the meaning of this phrase? Consider all this in light of the initial inquiry in verse 13.

_____

_____

_____

_____

_____

THE WATCHFUL SERVANTS + THE ABSENT HOMEOWNER

Pray that Jesus would help you learn to serve him with your whole life.

Read and reflect on Mark 13:33–37 and Luke 12:35–40.

How does the Parable of the Watchful Servants (Luke 12:35–40) help explain the Parable of the Absent Homeowner (Mark 13:33–37)? What is the main theme of both parables?

_____

_____

_____

What is the same about the parables and what is different?

_____

_____

_____

What do these parables indicate about what it means to live as a member of the kingdom of God (or kingdom of heaven)? What does a member of the kingdom of heaven *do* (and not do)? Consider that Jesus told these parables during his last journey to Jerusalem, when he knew he would be crucified and soon no longer be with his disciples in person.

_____

_____

_____

Read Luke 12:13–21, the Parable of the Rich Fool. How does that parable relate to the Parable of the Watchful Servants (12:35–40)? Note that the only gap between these parables is Jesus' further explanation of the Parable of the Rich Fool (12:22–34). (Consider your insights from Lesson 1.) How does the Parable of the Rich Fool explain the meaning of the Parable of the Watchful Servants?

_____

_____

_____

In the Parable of the Watchful Servants, the "Son of Man" is Jesus (Luke 12:40). In this context, the expression refers to when he will return to earth. In light of this, what does Jesus want his followers to do *now*, before that time comes?

_____

_____

_____

THE FAITHFUL SERVANT AND THE WICKED SERVANT

Pray that Jesus will show you what he has entrusted you to do.

Read and reflect on Matthew 24:45–51 and Luke 12:41–48.

Read Matthew 24:36–44. In light of these verses, what is the meaning of the Parable of the Faithful Servant and Wicked Servant (Matt 24:45–51)?

_____

_____

_____

What does the wise and faithful servant do for his fellow servants (24:45–47)?

_____

_____

_____

How does the master respond to him? How will Jesus respond to those who rise to the occasion that he calls them to?

_____

_____

_____

What are the characteristics of the wicked servant (24:48–51)? What are the ultimate results of his actions?

_____

_____

_____

Read James 3:1. If Jesus calls us to a certain area of ministry (such as leadership or teaching), what does he expect of us? What happens when we take for granted what he has given us (Matt 24:51; Luke 12:48)? (Note that the master is not just upset because of what the servant *hasn't* done, but he is also angered by how the servant abuses the time he has been given—which ultimately hurts his fellow servants.)

_____

_____

_____

In the context of Luke's Gospel, the Parable of the Faithful Servant and Wicked Servant (Luke 12:41–48) is essentially an extension of the Parable of the Watchful Servants (12:35–40). (Compare Lesson 2.) Jesus is elaborating on the difference between faithful, wise behavior *and* foolish, selfish, wicked behavior. In light of this explanation, what does Jesus expect of his followers?

_____

_____

_____

THE TEN VIRGINS

 Pray that Jesus would help you be prepared to serve in his kingdom.

 Read and reflect on Matthew 25:1–13.

In Matthew's Gospel, the Parable of the Ten Virgins (25:1–13) directly follows the Parable of the Faithful Servant and Wicked Servant (24:45–51); there is no break in Jesus' speech. This means that Jesus is elaborating on the same thought. (Compare Weeks Two and Three.) What do these two parables have in common? What's different?

Keep in mind that Jesus is in no way endorsing the man's decision to have multiple wives; Jesus is reflecting on an analogy from his ancient Near Eastern context. Also note that Jesus' parables do not always equate God the Father or himself with particular figures—and he certainly isn't doing so in this parable. It's not making a direct analogy, but rather illustrating a point (compare Matt 7:9–11).

Think about the Parable of the Ten Virgins (Matt 25:1–13) in light of three other parables:

- The Faithful Servant and Wicked Servant (Matt 24:45–51; Luke 12:41–48);

- The Watchful Servants (Luke 12:35–40);

- The Absent Homeowner (Mark 13:33–37).

What do all four parables have in common?

_____

_____

_____

In the Parable of the Faithful Servant and Wicked Servant (Matt 24:45–51), both servants are making an intentional choice about what type of person they want to be. Is the same true in the Parable of the Ten Virgins (25:1–13)? What do these two parables say about the various ways people respond to the kingdom of heaven?

_____

_____

_____

Read Matthew 7:15–23. How does Jesus distinguish his followers from everyone else (compare Matt 25:31–46)? What should be our response to Jesus (25:13)? What type of people should we be?

_____

_____

_____

THE TALENTS +
THE TEN MINAS

Pray that the Holy Spirit would help you to properly use the resources God has given you.

Read and reflect on Matthew 25:14–30 and Luke 19:11–27.

In the Parable of the Talents (Matt 25:14–30), the first servant is given the equivalent of 75 years' worth of wages; the second servant receives 30 years' worth of wages; and the third servant, 15 years' worth. The master is giving them money to steward while he is away, based on his perception of what they can handle appropriately.

What do the first two servants do with their money (25:16–17)? What is the result of their actions (25:19–23)?

_____

_____

_____

What does the third servant do with his money (25:18)? What is the result of his actions (Matt 25:24–30)?

_____

_____

_____

Are we to live in fear of God or take action? What type of risks does God expect us to take? As you read these parables, keep in mind that Jesus is not portraying God the Father like the managers. He is simply using an analogy about the way people act and comparing it to God's expectations.

_____

_____

_____

Read Matthew 25:31–46, which comes right after the Parable of the Talents. In light of this passage, how are we to use the resources Jesus has entrusted to us? What does this passage say about how a member of the kingdom of heaven lives?

_____

_____

_____

What is the difference between the Parable of the Talents (Matt 25:14-30) and the Parable of the Ten Minas (Luke 19:11-27)? (A mina was a weight of currency equal to about three months' wages.)

_____

_____

_____

In both parables, the third servant finishes with the same amount he was given at the start. Why is even that small amount taken away (Matt 25:28-30; Luke 19:24-27)? What does that say about Jesus' expectations—in terms of our gifts, skills, resources, and what's entrusted to our leadership?

_____

_____

_____

THE WEDDING FEAST + THE GREAT BANQUET

Pray that God would help you to fully accept his invitation for your life.

Read and reflect on Luke 14:7–24.

To understand the context of this parable, read Luke 14:1–6. In light of these verses, what issue is Jesus addressing in the Parable of the Wedding Feast (14:7–11)? Jesus has just healed a man, but the Pharisees are concerned with something else. What does Jesus' commentary throughout 14:7–24 say about their concerns (and humility in general)?

_____

_____

_____

Does the dinner guest who speaks in Luke 14:15 understand the purpose of what Jesus says in 14:12–14 (and before that in his parable)? If not, how does the guest misunderstand Jesus?

_____

_____

_____

In light of Jesus' audience (14:1–3) and his comments to the dinner's host (14:12–14), what issue is Jesus addressing in the Parable of the Great Banquet (14:15–24)?

_____

_____

_____

What is God inviting each of us to do? What happens when we excuse away
God's invitation (14:23-24)?

_____

_____

_____

Read Luke 14:25-35. What does Jesus' teaching in these verses have to do with
the two parables he tells at the dinner with the Pharisees (14:7-24)? What does
Jesus expect members of the kingdom of heaven to do? How should we react
when we are told God's plan for our lives?

_____

_____

_____

THE PRINCE'S WEDDING FEAST

Pray that God would help you respond appropriately to his love—and to celebrate it.

Read and reflect on Matthew 22:1–14.

What are the similarities and differences between the Parable of the Prince's Wedding Feast (Matt 22:1–14) and the Parable of the Great Banquet (Luke 14:15–24)? (These two parables are distinctly different, but certainly parallel.)

_____

_____

_____

Read Matthew 21:28–44. What do these parables—the Two Sons (21:28–32) and the Tenant Farmers (21:33–44)—have in common with the Parable of the Prince's Wedding Feast (22:1–14)? What does this teach about how we should respond to God's invitation to join him in his wondrous works (his actions in the world)?

_____

_____

_____

In Matthew 22:12–13, there is an incident with a man who decides to accept the king's invitation, but does not wear proper wedding attire. The problem is what his attire indicates: a lack of care for the king, the king's son, and the occasion. The man is there to benefit from the event, not to serve the king or celebrate his son. In light of this—and the larger context of people rejecting the king's invitation completely—what's the meaning of Matthew 12:14? What's the application in our lives?

_____

_____

_____

What does the Parable of the Prince's Wedding Feast teach us about how most people will respond to God as Father and God as Jesus? How should we respond?

_____

_____

_____

THE WORKERS IN THE VINEYARD

Pray that Jesus would show you the true meaning of justice and transform your perspective.

Read and reflect on Matthew 20:1–16.

Jesus delivered this parable during his ministry in Judea, earlier in his ministry than the parables in our last seven lessons. What does this context indicate about the meaning of the Parable of the Workers in the Vineyard (Matt 20:1–16)?

_____

_____

_____

A denarius is the equivalent of a full day's pay for a common laborer. This means the people who worked a full day received a *full day's* pay. In light of this, what does their reaction say about their view of justice and fairness (20:1–12)?

_____

_____

_____

What is the kingdom of heaven *like* in light of this parable (20:1, 13)? How should the kingdom of heaven change your paradigm of forgiveness?

_____

_____

_____

Read the Parable of the Two Debtors (Luke 7:41–48). What does it share in common with the Parable of the Workers in the Vineyard (Matt 20:1–16)? What's different? (Think about what is given in one and forgiven in the other, and what it symbolizes.) What is the one thing that everyone can receive from Jesus (John 3:16–17; Acts 4:11–12; Eph 1:3–14)?

_____

_____

_____

How should we view ourselves as members of the kingdom of heaven? How do we compare to others, and what should be our approach to life (Matt 20:14–16)?

_____

_____

_____

CONCLUSION

To understand God, you have to *experience* a relationship with him. In his parables, Jesus is essentially saying to us, "Those under God's reign *live like this*." The kingdom of heaven is mysterious, like God himself, but it can be *experienced*.

PART 4

THE KINGDOM TRANSFORMS OUR WORLD

The old adage that book smarts can't replace street smarts is also true when it comes to Jesus' parables. You cannot simply study them; you have to live them.

Jesus' parables reveal the secrets of the kingdom of heaven, while also leaving the kingdom enigmatic. Ultimately they show that God's reign is not something we can ever fully grasp. We can only *understand* the mystery of heaven as we *live* its values.

It's for these reasons that Jesus spoke in parables, which are extended metaphors or similes. (For Jesus' explanation of parables, see Matt 13:10–17, 34–35.) Jesus tells us that those who will understand these stories are those who choose to live their message—those who choose to follow the way of the kingdom of heaven (Jesus' way). The parables show us the principles of the kingdom of heaven and how it's manifested on earth.

In these eight lessons, we will examine a series of parables Jesus taught during his last journey to Jerusalem. We will then look at two parables he gave during his last days in Jerusalem, just before his crucifixion. We will see what it means to embrace Jesus, who suffered on our behalf for our salvation. We will learn what God expects of us—and how fulfilling those expectations can change our world.

THE LOST COIN

Pray that Jesus would show you how much he values your life—and the lives of others.

Read Luke 15:1–10. Then reflect slowly on Luke 15:8–10.

In what ways does the Parable of the Lost Sheep (Luke 15:1–7) explain the Parable of the Lost Coin (15:8–10)? What's thematically the same about both parables? What's celebrated in each—and *how* are those things celebrated (15:6–7, 9–10)?

_____

_____

_____

Jesus tells these parables during his last journey to Jerusalem (before his death on the cross). In light of this, what do you think he is preparing his disciples to do (15:10)?

_____

_____

_____

What social commentary is Jesus offering to his audience (15:1–2)? What is Jesus' view of the downtrodden and those who are far from God? What is Jesus' view of the religious establishment of his day?

_____

_____

_____

What is the value God places on the life of each and every person (15:10)? What does he do when one person is lost? What is his goal for all people?

_____

_____

_____

THE LOST SON

Pray that Jesus would reveal to you the ways you are lost.

Read and reflect on Luke 15:11–32.

What mistakes does the lost son make—in his perceptions of his father and of wealth, and in his actions (Luke 15:11–19)? Consider that Jews in Jesus' day did not eat pork or even touch pigs (which were considered unclean). In light of this, how did the lost son feel (15:15–16)? Also consider the famine that comes on the land: How did that influence his situation (15:14)?

_____

_____

_____

What's the best decision the lost son makes (15:17–19)? Remember that he had no idea how his father would react. He seems to indicate that he is merely requesting to be received as a servant, not a son.

_____

_____

_____

In Luke 15:31–32, what do the father's words indicate about the response of the older son? What mistakes does the older son make?

_____

_____

_____

Jesus is illustrating a principle of the kingdom of heaven in the Parable of the Lost Son (or Prodigal Son). What does this parable indicate about the different ways people respond to the kingdom of heaven?

_____

_____

_____

Compare the Parable of the Lost Son (Luke 15:11–19) to the Parable of the Two Debtors (Luke 7:41–48) and the Parable of the Workers in the Vineyard (Matt 20:1–16). How do these other parables make sense of the Parable of the Lost Son?

_____

_____

_____

How should we respond to the kingdom of heaven? How should we view our day-to-day relationship with Jesus?

_____

_____

_____

THE DISHONEST MANAGER

Pray that God would show you the proper way to steward your resources and conduct business.

Read Luke 16:1–15. Then slowly reflect on Luke 16:1–13.

When Jesus offers a parable, he is not necessarily equating God the Father or himself with particular figures in the parable. Instead, he is offering an analogy based on common experiences in the ancient Near East. In Luke 16:1–13, Jesus addresses how the wealthy and dishonest deal with cashflow issues and the potential loss of a job. In light of this, what is Jesus saying about how things in the world generally work? What does the manager do that is dishonest (or unethical)? What does he seem to know about the man he works for (16:1–9)? (Is it possible that Jesus is being sarcastic in 16:9?)

_____

_____

_____

Right after this parable comes the Parable of the Rich Man and Lazarus (16:19–31). The only thing in between is Jesus' discussion with a group of Pharisees (religious leaders of the time; 16:14–18). What does this further discussion indicate about the meaning of the Parable of the Dishonest Manager (16:1–9)? What does the Parable of the Rich Man and Lazarus (16:19–31) indicate about the meaning of the Parable of the Dishonest Manager and its explanation (16:1–13)?

_____

_____

_____

How does Jesus expect us to handle wealth—and finances in general (16:10-11)?

_____

_____

_____

Jesus' questions in Luke 16:11-12 do not indicate that he endorses the behavior of the manager. Instead, the parable illustrates how a person who values wealth will do whatever it takes to maintain that wealth (even act dishonestly). What is Jesus saying about the difference between a person who values the kingdom of heaven and a person who values wealth (16:13)? How do their ethics differ (16:1-9)? What (or who) does a member of the kingdom serve?

_____

_____

_____

THE RICH MAN AND LAZARUS

Pray that Jesus would give you a deep love and empathy for the impoverished.

Read and reflect on Luke 16:19–31.

What does the discussion in Luke 16:14–18 indicate about the meaning of the Parable of the Rich Man and Lazarus (16:19–31)? What specific issues and attitudes in society is Jesus commenting on?

_____

_____

_____

How does the rich man react to Lazarus? What does this show about his character and values (16:19–21)? In what ways do we react similarly to suffering?

_____

_____

_____

What is the ultimate fate of Lazarus? What is the ultimate fate of the rich man (Luke 16:22–23)? What does the rich man's call to Abraham—the forefather of the Jewish people (Gen 12:1–9)—indicate about how his views have changed (Luke 16:24)?

_____

_____

_____

What does Abraham's response to the rich man indicate about repentance (the need to change our ways) and God's expectations (Luke 16:25-26)? When confronted with God's saving message (John 3:16-17), how should we react? What if we don't change our ways and embrace God's ways?

_____

_____

_____

What do Abraham's final words indicate about how God communicates with the world—and the overall response to God's saving message (Luke 16:27-31)?

_____

_____

_____

Based on the Parable of the Rich Man and Lazarus (Luke 16:19-31), what are some tangible ways people show that they are members of the kingdom of heaven? How does Jesus recognize his true followers (compare Matt 25:31-46)? How then should you change your ways?

_____

_____

_____

THE UNWORTHY SERVANTS

Pray that the Holy Spirit would help you adopt an attitude of complete humility.

Read Luke 17:1–10. Then reflect slowly on Luke 17:7–10.

What does Luke 17:1–6 indicate about the meaning of the parable in 17:7–10?

_____

_____

_____

The Parable of the Unworthy Servants (17:7–10) comes shortly after the Parable of the Rich Man and Lazarus (16:19–31). What do these parables have in common—especially in light of Jesus' teaching between the parables (17:1–6)?

_____

_____

_____

Consider that Luke 17:1–6 focuses on the "little ones" (children, who were often marginalized in Jesus' day). What does marginalizing the helpless have to do with both parables? What do these parables say about our perceptions of our wealth and status?

_____

_____

_____

What does Jesus' teaching in Luke 17:3-4—and his conclusion to the Parable of the Unworthy Servants (17:10)—indicate about how we should respond to the forgiveness God offers us? (Note that Jesus is not endorsing the behavior in the parable, but instead using this common occurrence in the ancient Near East to illustrate how we should respond to the God of the universe, to whom we owe everything.)

_____

_____

_____

Consider Jesus' teaching in Luke 17:5-6, which addresses the power of faith. What does the theme of faith have to do with the Parable of the Unworthy Servants (17:7-10)? How do members of the kingdom of God respond to their master? What should be their expectations and mindset (attitude)?

_____

_____

_____

THE PERSISTENT WIDOW + THE PHARISEE AND THE TAX COLLECTOR

Ask the Holy Spirit to teach you how to pray earnestly and in humility.

Read and reflect on Luke 18:1–14.

Luke 18:1 defines the purpose of the Parable of the Persistent Widow (18:1–7; also called the Parable of the Unjust Judge). This is one of the few places where the narrator directly tells us the reason why Jesus offers a particular parable.

In the Parable of the Persistent Widow, what are Jesus' two main points (18:6–8)?

_____

_____

_____

_____

What should we do in light of this teaching?

_____

_____

_____

As in Luke 18:1, the narrator explains in 18:9 why Jesus tells the next parable. What point is illustrated by the Parable of the Pharisee and the Tax Collector (18:10–14)?

_____

_____

_____

If you were to summarize how Jesus expects us to live in three or four sentences, what would you say?

_____

_____

_____

_____

THE TWO SONS

Pray that God would teach you how to truly repent, even after you've made a mistake.

Read Matthew 21:23–32. Then reflect slowly on Matthew 21:28–32.

What does Matthew 21:23–27 indicate about the meaning of the Parable of the Two Sons (21:28–32)? (Note that there is no break in Jesus' speech from verse 27 to verse 28; his discussion with the religious leaders flows directly into the parable.) What norms is Jesus challenging? What is he saying about his own identity and how people view him?

_____

_____

_____

In what ways do you live like the first son (21:28–29)? In what ways do you act like the second son (21:30–31)?

_____

_____

_____

How does God hope we will respond to the opportunity to do his will?

_____

_____

_____

In Matthew 21:31, Jesus explains the meaning of the Parable of the Two Sons. In what ways does your life resemble that of the religious leaders who rejected Jesus (like the second son in the parable)? In what ways do you consider yourself religiously "right"?

_____

_____

_____

Read Matthew 3:1–12. Now consider Matthew 21:32 and how the religious leaders didn't understand Jesus (but thought they did). In what ways do you think your life is correctly showing the values of the kingdom of heaven? In what ways are you *not* living those values? How are you misjudging others— and ultimately misjudging God's will? What needs to change?

_____

_____

_____

THE TENANT FARMERS

Pray that Jesus would open your eyes and heart to the presence of his kingdom.

Read Mark 12:1–12 and Luke 20:9–19. Reflect on Matthew 21:33–46.

In Matthew's Gospel, the Parable of the Two Sons (Matt 21:28–32) occurs right before the Parable of the Tenant Farmers (21:33–40). What point do both parables make? Consider this question especially in light of the setting of both parables—the Jerusalem Temple in front of Jewish religious leaders (21:23–27).

_____

_____

_____

Who do the servants represent in the Parable of the Tenant Farmers (Matt 21:33–36)? Who does the son represent (21:37–39)?

_____

_____

_____

Considering Matthew 21:41–45, read Psalm 118:22–23 (which Jesus is quoting). Then read Acts 4:5–12 and 1 Peter 2:4–8. What do these other passages suggest about the meaning of the Parable of the Tenant Farmers (Matt 21:33–40)?

_____

_____

_____

How do the religious leaders ultimately respond to Jesus (Matt 21:45–46)? (Note that in Matthew 21:43, Jesus is specifically addressing Jewish *religious leaders*, not all Jewish people. Remember, Jesus and his disciples were Jewish, too.)

_____

_____

_____

What will happen when someone hears Jesus' message and completely rejects it, without ever changing their mind in the future (Matt 21:44)?

_____

_____

_____

Consider this parable in light of Jesus' suffering, crucifixion, and resurrection (Matt 26:47–28:20). What is the ultimate result of Jesus' suffering, death, and resurrection? What opportunity does Jesus' sacrificial death and resurrection give us? How does it make the presence of the kingdom of heaven (God's reign) possible in our lives and world?

_____

_____

_____

CONCLUSION

Jesus asks us to embrace the kingdom of heaven, even if we're not sure what it all means. The parables prompt us to embrace the crucified and resurrected Messiah, Jesus. They prompt us to embrace the presence of God's kingdom here on earth; to hope for the day when Jesus will return and make all things right; and to proclaim his message in the meantime.

Jesus' parables show us what it means to be his followers, who are empowered by the Holy Spirit to walk in his ways and make our world a better place. Go and live as a member of God's kingdom. Embrace the wonder and beauty of his reign in every aspect of your life.

ABOUT THE AUTHOR

John D. Barry is a nonprofit CEO, Bible scholar, and pastor. After a career in Christian publishing and Bible software, John and his wife, Kalene, sold their house and nearly everything they owned to dedicate their lives to Jesus' Economy, an innovative nonprofit creating jobs and churches in the developing world. John and Kalene also serve as missionaries with Resurrect Church Movement, the domestic division of Jesus' Economy, equipping US churches to effectively alleviate poverty and bring people to Jesus.

John is the general editor of the highly acclaimed *Faithlife Study Bible* and *Lexham Bible Dictionary*, which are used by over one million people, and the author or editor of thirty books, including the popular daily devotional *Connect the Testaments* and multiple Not Your Average Bible Study volumes. John formerly served as publisher of Lexham Press and editor-in-chief of *Bible Study Magazine*.

In a primarily unchurched area of the United States, John has worked extensively with the homeless, helped plant a church, and launched a ministry. Internationally, John has initiated indigenous church planting efforts and the drilling of water wells and launched an online fair trade marketplace (to empower the impoverished). He speaks internationally on engaging the Bible, poverty, and spreading the gospel. John's latest book is *Jesus' Economy: A Biblical View of Poverty, the Currency of Love, and a Pattern for Lasting Change*. Learn more at JesusEconomy.org.